DAWN PASSAGES

DAWN PASSAGES

Poems of
Death and Resurrection

ANITAH L. GOMBOS

LUMINARE PRESS

WWW.LUMINAREPRESS.COM

Luminare Press
438 Charnelton St., Suite 101
Eugene, OR 97401
www.luminarepress.com

LCCN: 2018947202
ISBN: 978-1-944733-88-9

*With great thanks and gratitude, this book is
dedicated to my family, friends, and contrarians, both
seen and unseen, whose love, support, and challenges have
brought me to this miraculous moment.*

You know who you are.

Table of Contents

Introduction

DEATH CAN TAKE MANY FORMS—ALL KINDS OF END-ings, partings, and events which cause us to mourn a significant loss. Physical death. The death of a relationship. The death of something familiar. Anyone or anything pushing us into the dark and unknown can bring a type of death. The death of a loved one, however, is monumental and unlike any other.

When someone we love dies, the world around us changes. We change. Tumbling about with death, pain and separation can cruelly twist our hearts and scour our souls, no matter how grounded we are in knowing life continues and no matter how peaceful or welcomed the final passing. We miss our loved one. Our human hearts hurt.

However, if we travel death's pathways with greater understanding and acceptance, we can stand at the threshold of eternity itself and be initiated into deeper mysteries. Death invites us to remember we are immortal and will never be snuffed out. Love, a bond even death cannot break, holds firm.

Even though it can be confusing and terrible, death is a sacred time—despite how temporarily contorted we become in our aloneness. We forget the mortal pact we unconsciously made with life when we were born—that upon entering death's dim halls after a loved one dies, we would again seek the light and resurrect to new life. This passage is always ours to accept or deny. However, choosing by default to remain in death's underworld can bring about our own inner death and disintegration.

Within us lies the map to make this journey. We need only remember how to access it. That's what these poems are all about.

Death is not a once-and-done event, but a tide taking us far into the deep before bringing us back to ourselves in wave after wave of difficult, and often contradictory, emotions before the waters calm and return us to center once again. Love becomes the anchor keeping us from becoming unmoored and unfound.

Death is a time of transition, a link between what-was and what-is-yet-to-be. Death, then, is the co-creator of life.

In Eastern traditions, Kali, the wellspring of death and destruction, is the consort of Shiva, the creator and life-giver. Death clears the way and makes room for life—always—just as forest fires clear the ground for long-dormant seeds to grow. In the West, with our binary way of dividing everything into either/or categories like good/bad and dark/light, we place a positive spin on life and a negative on death. But this viewpoint takes us far from the roots of our shared humanity.

Like most, I have experienced many forms of death, but, for me, the death of my father ten years after my mother died, required an unexpectedly different journey. The passing of his generation and a more profound recognition of my own mortality rocked me. Though I had the comfort of family and friends, I was propelled onto a solitary path, creating a new backdrop for the very way I viewed life and the role I played on this planet. Shiva eventually emerged, but first there was Kali.

I consider the time I had with my father before he died to be one of the greatest gifts of my life. I remain most grateful for the opportunity we had to know each other as adults and interesting people—beyond traditional father-daughter roles. Dad became a friend and my biggest fan.

My father's death unsettled my world—even more than the sudden death decades before of the man I thought I would marry. This man's death when still so young was out-of-time and unusual, but with my father's passing, I realized my generation was next-in-line on the approach to death's door. More profoundly, *I* was next in line. With this shift in perspective, all the deaths I had ever experienced—physical, emotional, psychological—flooded back, demanding to be reexamined and given more consequential meaning.

I wrote these poems about my own travel with death before, during, and after my father's passing, but I never thought I would publish them. They are highly personal and chronicle my inner process of death and resurrection when Dad's physical life ended. However, when I gave a few poems to those facing death's loss, it helped them put words around their own experiences. So, I began sharing my poems with more friends. Since meaning-making is central to how humans engage in life and with each other, I hope offering them more broadly may help those who are trying to make sense of what might feel like a senseless time.

When I was growing up, I feared death—scared that death would take away those I loved and shatter the safe space in which I dwelled. Now I understand death as part of the process of growth and change, a prelude to expansion and creation. Death made me ponder how a seed must first break open before making its journey through soil's darkness and density—reaching for the sun, taking in water and nourishment, finally unfolding into light. Was this not my process as well? During death's transition, the balming love of those who held me close and encouraged me to come back into the light, gave me the courage to emerge from my personal darkness. But first death broke open my heart.

Poems wrap words around an experience, an expression of life, sometimes with a literal rendering and at other times, more abstractly. Poetry's images are often the stuff of dreams and profound connection with the Other—with someone or something inviting us to become more than we imagine ourselves to be. Poetry, with great impact, can speak to both the mortal and immortal aspects of self and the sacred union of both. It reminds us of our true shared humanity.

However, no matter the form, the words of poetry deliver *energy packets*—pockets of meaning—slipping below the logic of the conscious mind to root and grow in the mind's deeper strata where, hidden, they can eventually flower and infuse us with vitality. Maturing in their season, they then produce fruits of new meaning.

Since my father began his death journey in the fall, many of the poems reference and parallel seasonal changes. The poems written during this process reflect his decline in early autumn; his continued descent throughout winter bringing his death at its end; the blossoming in spring of my nascent hope; and a tentative return to full living in the summer months. The seasons made his passing much more meaningful for me as Earth fittingly mirrored my inner states. Earth and I made this journey together.

Poetry is meant to open and be read by the heart, especially these poems of death and resurrection. Often, meaning is found in the in-between where eternal truths dwell, and secrets hidden in plain sight are there for those willing to find and be found. In-between letters, words, and lines. In-between heaven and earth.

Remain mindful of this as you sink into these poems. They progress from twilight—the dimming of the day, the drawing near of death—through nighttime and dawn, until daylight reveals the potentials of a richer, truer life.

May these poems help you more easily pilot your own dark passages as you make the journey through death towards promised resurrection.

Anitah Gombos,
June 6, 2018

TWILIGHT

TWILIGHT

WILLINGLY EMBRACING LIFE'S DIFFICULT, AND OFTEN inevitable, transitions is never easy and not for the faint of heart. These times, when endurance and steadfast faith might be difficult to hold onto, test the soul. They can sometimes even feel impossible to find. Questions pound. How can I possibly get to the other side of this? What does this all mean? Will everything and everyone be okay?

But these are also crucible times of tempering fire, when you are forged with greater strength and resilience. When death initially breaks open your heart, only pain and doubt erupt from the deepest parts of you. However, over time, these early feelings can give way to life-changing emotions, as death stretches your heart and makes room for more love, acceptance, and gratitude.

Death's transitions are times of the soul, when you are invited to come home to yourself in a new way. You can and will survive death. But simply getting through your grief is not enough for the transformation this passage offers. Awareness, humility, and compassion for yourself and others, like the process of ancient alchemy, change the lead of outdated beliefs into the gold of greater wisdom. You move closer to becoming more conscious and truer as you respond differently to the everyday ordinary.

Death's tough transition initiated at twilight sometimes begins with questioning. You can feel off-balance, not quite understanding where this situation will lead you. You sense a big change is coming, and you are forced to view your usual life differently from what you have known as constant and real.

Sometimes, the coming death transition shadows your inner world and, suspecting what is to come, you feel the chill of difficult change. However, like reading the last chapter of a suspense novel to be sure your favorite characters survive, activating your innate soul-gift of hope offers assurances at the beginning of death's transition that if you stay the course, you will be unbroken when you arrive at its end, no matter how confounding the journey might get and no matter how dark it becomes. Hope sheds a light.

Active hope operates as an internal GPS taking you safely across death's stormy waters and safely into port. Though like the tides on which it travels, hope can ebb and flow. Ebb times call for another soul-gift—faith. Faith in yourself, in others, and in your process. Flow times are for standing in gratitude with the unshakeable trust that love will find a way.

On some days, you might rail against what is to come. On others, you find a bit of peace. Tides. Ebbs and flows. Metaphorically, the sun can even offer a final burst of bright light, and your loved one seems on the road to recovery. You perhaps feel like all your misgivings were part of a nasty dream, until you realize you are not asleep and the pain mockingly returns. This is all part of the mysteried process of creation and transformation—the eternal process of clearing away and fashioning the new.

If you have the courage to begin the journey as the navigating captain and not default to the role of desperate passenger, salvation comes at the completion of the voyage, and you find you've been remade. Initiation begins in the unquiet of twilight as you begin the rhythmic cycle of life and move in the stepped pattern of death's make-sacred dance.

Twilight

The spiraling circle of soul's true cycle
Brings me again to completion's shedding
Mimicking autumn's long exhale.

Driven by season's stilling needs
I retreat to a shadowed inner cave
Prepared by introspective caution
For winter's pretend hibernation.

Releasing summer's lugubrious pace
With all its sensuous frivolities
I encase myself in tutorial wool
A defense from the coming gloom.

I settle and sink more deeply
Into the chill of darkening nights
Where only a warming tending fire
With flickering pledge of returning light
Can take me safely into spring.

When called forth by its clocked command
I will once again dance with wild abandon
Through blooming miles of poppied meadows
Clad only in new life's spangled delight
In promises made and kept.

Cold Morning

White roof crackling with brittle frost
Mirrors the softened glide of illumined hawk.

I breathe air as promising as newly voiced vows
And tremble at the unspoken question.

Lifting In

It is not the return to indigenous state
Now navigating beckoning spirit
But the fundamental yearning of my frosted heart
To resonate again with the warming breath
Of creation's original chord.

The soul-signature of my known-deep destiny
Beyond this time and space
Awaits its augured reclamation
Through the sacramental transmutation
Of quickening heaven and conjoining earth
As ascending in angel-like tonal precision
In progressive multi-finality
I surrender to the seductive aromatics
Of eternity's sacred song.

The Turn of Seasons

I like the softness of summer's darkness
The gradual glad leaving of the sun
As Earth releases her embracing warmth
And stars invite my courtship.

Only in near-winter do I burn more lights
This time of the longer nights
When I surround my wary recoiling senses
In a close bright womb of circled illumination
A walled frontier of safety and belonging.

As cutting cold mercilessly enshrouds
The shivering and now-stilled land,
Shadows call forth ancient remembrance
Of nocturnal terror in tempest-tossed caves
Of snapping predators howling for blood.

In this no-moment of illusory evolution
Of civilization's pretend protection
I become more mortal and forebodingly afraid
Cellular fear demands sacrifice and satiation
To keep the unquiet at bay.

So, on an altar of my own undoing
I feed the old gods the steaming gore
Of my gut-incised presumptions
Then quietly await in the redemptive dark
For the wind-chased moans to end.

Days Between

What happens when the words don't come
When the usual singing surge of lapping images
Withdraw unilaterally in pre-tsunami retrograde
Leaving bare and bereft on the sandy shores
The gasping fish of silvered expression?

How do I prepare for the returning turmoil?

Do I safely retreat to higher ground
And use distance for protection?
Or do I stand on the bleeding shoreline
And invite the world to balance?

I really don't know what to do
So, in the in-between of this moment
I will simply remain quite still
While mutely awaiting the tumult
Of a flattening incoming tide.

Beyond

Is it the wind making the tall trees sing
Or the trees giving wind full expression?

Do the rain and sun create the ever rainbows
Or do the rainbows give purpose to their alliance?

Projected onto this lovely planet
We are tricks of light and dust
And so, I ask in respectful query
Who is the dreamer and who the dreamed
And who, the rainbowed wind?

Surge

Bounded tears surge inside me
For these old ones awaiting death
So much a part of my growing-up cycle
Now nearing the completion of their days
When my cache of tears will tumble out
In love
In gratitude
In missing moments.

I feel the fragility of this human game
We so willingly play with each other
Pretending it is the only real.

But we're eternity's sparks clothed in human dust
Glorying in our brief moments of hallowed touch
Enjoying the panoply of the dancing God-lights
We have come to know as friends.

I will miss him.

Reprieve

Like kind candlelight on leathered faces
The fog softens my deeply etched boundaries
And blurs the not-ever-good-enough lines
Of hard and loveless places
Allowing me to temporarily forget
The cruel unanswerable questions
Of my increasingly tensioned heart.

Ripening

I could not find him in this polite and passive man.

This larger-than-life grand figure
Whose jettisoning energy
Fetched both delightful interplay
And resigned admiration
Has gone far away
Deep inside
"To get my mind around this place," he said
This dreaded diminishing space
Of stunning incapacity.

I hope he comes back.

I hope he knows I no longer require
Molehills-to-mountains extravagance
What now suffices are meandering chats
With their familiar downy comfort.

I hope after emotionally mapping
This frontier of fate's harsh design
He can feed on new hope
And when sated by time
He might free his bound-tight spirit.

Malaise

The rhythm of my saddened soul
Keeps pace with fall's slow dirge
As the last bright leaves of this drifting season
Fade fitfully in carpeting brown.

This, the dreaded time of seeping silence
Of light depressed by snow-blanked clouds
When songbirds flee to warmer hills
And the quivered heart beats erratic alarm
Coiled tightly against the plaintive cry
Of the last goose winging away.

Trust

With feathers fluffed against the cold
This little one with tucked-in wings
Like all of us who face night's chill
Awaits the warming breath of dawn.

Exploration

Like a starship bouncing off planet's atmosphere
To boost acceleration and momentum
I utilize the vivifying thrust of life's every event
To find entry into deeper space.

Departed Family

In the pageanted fall when bright colors abound
I miss them most
Loved ones gone into the gray
Who now feel so terribly absent.

The familiar summer heat no longer presses
Like the unceasing devotion of a faithful dog
Nor does it envelope and embrace me in the night
Like the whispered touch of a lover.

Instead I feel the chill begin
As I pile on cocooning layers
To hold the warmth for just a little longer
For another kindly while.

I repel the coming stalking cold
And stand readied for the remembering times
When the cruel cutting winds of all-aloneness
Mercilessly slash my heart.

NIGHT

NIGHT

NIGHTTIME FALLS, THE LEADING-TO-DEATH TIME, A dark wintry experience of letting go and already missing. Some people die slowly and there is a longer period of saying goodbye with its accompanying distress if they witness the pain and confusion of those deeply loved. For others, the quick jolt of departure leaves bewilderment and searing hurt behind. It is the way of things.

But for those of us who remain and mourn the loss, grief erupts from a heart broken open. Prepared or unprepared, we begin to walk death's path. We choose consciously, or by default, how we will make death's ancient passage—either with haste to get to the other side or by remaining present to this sacred journey—our inauguration into the deep transformative places where grief reveals a gift found only within a death-struck heart. Understanding that the wounding is a predictable step in death's dance can bring some measure of peace when hope and meaning-making feel distant.

The form and timing of mourning are different for everyone. Though death is a shared human experience, no one can fully comprehend or accurately judge what another person is feeling. Therefore, never accept the judgements or even the well-meaning counsel from loved ones about how to handle your grief if it doesn't feel right for you. Above all, do not justify or judge yourself. This is a very personal and potentially sacred time. There are no hard-and-fast rules about how to grieve. Mourning is the time to explore your own depths and excavate always-present wisdom.

Allow mourning to be messy. Let it take its time and run its course. You will sense when grief is ready to leave—when life challenges you to begin moving beyond death's initial wounding. Conversely, you may realize you have held onto your pain for far too long and have become trapped in self-indulgent mourning. If you feel stuck and cannot move beyond your grief, seek help. Death's transition challenges you to be courageous and give careful attention to both yourself and others. But reach out only to those who honor and respect you—who do not burden you with their own opinions about your journey.

Whether assistance comes from a loved one, a spiritual advisor, or a professional counsellor, listen. Accept their support. With help, you can care for the part of you that is confused and continues to hang onto how-life-used-to-be before death intruded—to move beyond initial grief and begin the passage to what-life-can-look-like-now with the healing of eternal grace.

However, when your heart begins to mend, it never returns to its former size. Instead, if you have kept faith with yourself, you find, Grinch-like, your heart has grown three sizes bigger. The divine patch sealing your slashed heart has been woven from the love you give to yourself and receive from others throughout death's journey. With time's remedy, the patch seamlessly becomes one with your heart and enlarges it, giving you a greater capacity to embrace life and welcome unexpected moments of blessing. This is your journey's end and the headwaters of your new future.

The shock of death can produce many different emotions during the dying process, especially when a loved one actually passes and the emptiness of missing them begins. Expect these very mortal emotions to come up so they don't surprise you, and you can begin making peace with them. Open to each of these feelings before moving beyond and letting it go. Anger, hate, relief, betrayal, doubt, love, confusion, regret, reproach—any and all are normal—all must be accepted and experienced. Do not judge this human cocktail of feelings presented in a chalice shaped by the pain of your wounded spirit. They are not to be denied. This brew, a divine medicine, is given for your restoration and can make you whole if you allow this elixir to do its work.

Integrating the death experience is a process others can talk about when offering their support, but no one can undertake it for you. Your walk with death is uniquely personal and solitary. After sinking into and clearing your initial distressing emotions, you begin to find meaning for this death, even when the death appears senseless. The process is not about asking the *why-me* questions which take you nowhere, but is about asking the *what-does-this-mean* questions eventually leading to enlightenment.

Again, death can be a sacred journey helping you become stronger and truer. Or, you can passively allow death to victimize you, wreck you, and take away part of your soul. It is always your choice. Always. You are stronger than you know. Make this true for you.

Night

I have always enjoyed the night
The embrace of dark
The shelter of silence
The communion with old, wise stars.

But the night has reshaped its contours
And distorted the familiar and safe.

Night.

Now a sinister playground
For unknown others
Taking pleasure in my terror.

They stalk me hungrily
With salivating zeal
Hastening their vile approach
Step by putrid step
Threatening my peace
Challenging my humanity.

I hear their vicious howling
And know they come for me.

I shudder in penetrating cold
And wonder why I am naked and alone
Twisting in tormented doubt
Terrified my path has disappeared.

Night.

Once a looking-forward-to time
Night is now the dread intruder
Severing me from my every possible.

Stripped, I am left with nothing
But this ripping pain of ending
And the panic of my own mortality.

Abandoned and forgotten
Bullied by the snapping threat of unseen predators
I fall bloodied and whimpering near a kindly tree
Which spreads its oaky roots to take me in
A guardian during this time of last lost innocence
A defense against what I sense is surely coming.

Sinking Up

The inky sky fills with cacophonous sound
As south-facing geese cry their winging way
"Fly with us—fly with us," they call
To yearning Earth-walking watchers.

I ache to accept their clamored offer
And longingly stretch my straining essence
Towards the freedom of moon-clad clouds
As my denser body sinks darkly into loss
Cruelly trapping my too-tendered heart
In unending near-death's pain.

Deeper
Deeper
Into the debilitating chill
Of cold death's cavernous underworld
Where hobgoblin minions greedily lick
The enervating pustules of mind's malaise
While stripping away my bewildered humanity
Of all but necessary functions.

But these are enough.

I will not fall
I will not disappear
I will not cease to be.

They cannot have me.

In the conceded dying of this year
I stand on the threshold of another ending
And trust the keepers of bounty's grace
To replace in full and plenty measure
The enormity being wrenched away.

I will trust time's life-supporting process
Through these predicted cycles of my soul
And await the ever-tidal turning
For spring's beckoned rebirthing.

And in this pause of fecund possibility
I will scan the cloudless star-kissed skies
For the first grand heart-gladdened glimpse
Of geese trumpeting their high-flying return
Demanding my bonded release.

Then scoured of dross by refashioning fires
I will set my kept-true spirit free
To rise undenied to the awaiting ones
And claim victorious completion.

Night

Interlude

As near-winter seduces the tiring autumn
A last butterfly feeling its chilling touch
Blows busily from one late bloom to next
From one baring branch to another.

I am saddened this awakened brightness
Will be extinguished by winter's cold
And imagine that his erratic flutters
Prefigure a fast-nearing end.

But this is simply not so.

This one will have it all before he goes
The sip of wind
The scent of moist
The kiss of kindly warmth.

It is not mortality which inspires his dance
But an honoring of time-misted vows
Made long ago to both Earth and her people
Taken by all freely binding themselves
To spend seasonal lives for this sacred land
Before surrendering to consecrating death.

Unquiet Tears

They are so very plentiful
My tears of seeping, separating grief
And these days ordinarily expected
Becoming the moment's what's-so.

They briefly cool erupting heat
From heartland's high emotion
Or explode from the unwalked depths
Of soul's unnamed profound.

Too hurriedly they're denied, dismissed
As profane and much too trite
Before time's circuitous river may run
To rightful and true redemption.

My refusals mindlessly misdirect
The beckoning parallel stream
Surging with the ebullient blessings
Of heaven's gifting grace

Then I hear the timeless caution.

Do not spend too readily
These salt-preserving tears
But reverently collect and hold them dear
Within the tension of changed perspective.

Let these bright refracting droplets
Wept by eyes still learning to see
Capture the sun of the rising possible
With its eternal rainbowed hope
Heaven's promise of new beginnings
When all unfolds as it should.

Listening, I bow to truth.

Deprivation

My eyes are hungry for the dawn.

My heart yearns for light's sustaining warmth
For the final banishing of constricting duality
For the social solitude of the One.

Monday's Child

I started to come apart that day
The tensile strength that held the harmony
Began hideously to unravel.

Like thin translucent porcelain
Dunked swiftly from boil to freeze,
Cracks abruptly began to surface
Along lines of inherent making.

Interminable chasms quaked and split
Pieces of who I thought myself to be
Spewed nastily and mockingly away.

Panicked that I would surely cease
I grabbed for them from my broken place
As they thundered darkly by
These sordid little contrivances
Which only I would want
These whimpers mewling for dispensation
These cacophonies clamoring for vindication
Made tragic by tenacious denial.

They liquefied my tentative ground
To an unholy quicksand of swamping terror
Greedily grabbing, atrociously sucking
Hurrying the fragile pieces left of me
Down the vile pit of forever desolation
To the safe-seeming womb of crazed oblivion.

Immersed in horrored disbelief
Contorted with tentacled destruction
I could do nothing but writhe and weep
While trusting in remaking survival.

Desertion

Pain is cold
It locks the limbs and shivers the heart
Coagulating crusted blood in frozen passageways.

Pain feels like death.

It brays like a penned-up hound
Tearing out the pulsing throat
Of lifetime's tender hope.

The Way of It All

Like a bitter surge of acid reflux
Following a thoroughly delightful meal
An unexpected eruption from my unconscious mind
Filled me with dread's most nasty bile
Of regurgitating, leftover issues
Dragging the focus of my now-bound attention
To farscaped payments come due.

"I cannot deal with you all," I cried
As in shocked and alarmed dismay
I stood quaking before this crowd.

"You are legion—you are too many," I moaned
As they grabbed my feet and began to climb
Up my ankles and over my calves
Up my knees and over my thighs
Poised to begin their battering advance
Toward the unprotected rest-of-me
Scrambling to reach even higher
In final killing assault.

Then I heard from one who always senses
Who smelled my distress in the spewing toxins
Filling the hundreds of miles between us.

"Be calm and believe," he quietly said
"Stop looking down and look forward again
 See what is possible—know what is true."

Not sensing his words had restored me
The hordes of old-stuff nano-nonsense
Continued their inexorable ascent
Ready to rip out my remedied heart.

But with sight unfrozen and voice now freed
I shouted ancient words of remembered power
To decisively cast down my thuggish progeny
Birthed from false fear's helpless lack.

"I trust! I trust! I forever trust!"
I repeated this trumpeting call
Again and again and always again
 Until with spell-casting innate authority
I finally articulated the magicked words
"I choose, and so it is."

My vow-breaks raced through titanic space
And vibrated along all-time's mutable threads
Delivering my choice to the weaver women
To re-loom my textured tapestried story
With patterns of the rediscovered.

In that exact same sacred moment
With an immediacy that halted my breath
The chattering cacophony was silenced and felled
Not going into hiding or threatening re-emergence
But sinking instead to the place of final resolution
To be inexorably buried with nevermore finality
In a tomb where old issues died.

In their decay, they feed mystery's deep-planted
    seeds
Awaiting their prophesized moment of emergence
While farmer-like I tend them in quieted darkness
And watch eagerly for the first hints of spring.

Tracings

Sometimes
After bruising hours of cryptic crying
I wish I could just let loose and wail
Setting free my gulping at-death tears
Ripped whole from the belly
Flung heedlessly from the soul.

How can these grave silent drippings
These pathetic petit-mal rivulets
Possibly ever suffice?

Then in a brightening stained-glass moment
I finally land the elusive insight
Wriggling in dark subterranean depths
Now leaping for understanding.

As garden's measured processional waters
Slowly irrigate rows of planted seeds
So, too, do these oozing timid tears
(And not ferocious volcanic eruptions)
More completely penetrate the deeper strata
Of my own fecund heartland
To slowly reawaken without startle or shock
My slumbering spring green urges.

March's Victims

It was just a pretending spring.

The warming sun shone seductively
And undercut my fierce defenses
My outer guaranteed protection
Against pillaging what-if thoughts.

Trusting, I shed this sheltering garb
And knew the joy of returned abandon.

I unfolded into the teasing light
And unwound from deep-night's darkness
Unfurling my greening hesitant buds
Into the swim of errant breeze.

Then the season returned.

The changing winds caught me unaware
As they shrieked down the troubled valley
Twisting torn branches into banshee shapes
Ripping me nastily from parent tree.

I lay wounded by fate
Crushed by darkness
Extinguished by cold
Suspended in the acidic surprise
Of death's perpetual perhaps.

When will the season truly turn?
When will I again feel the sun?
When will this pain finally end?
I ask with hurting resignation
As I return to my coated silence.

A Moment of Forever

Fumbling along the blind intersections
Of dark death's posturing details
Grief erupts.

It spews out thickly, unforgivingly
Arresting life's bright movement
In its murky capturing embrace.

Through eyes lost in wondering confusion
I watch as my secure foundation
Once resting firmly on the pleasantly familiar
Suddenly liquefies and melts away
In the ferocious heat of hurt.

Grief spreads messily and kills my comfort
And I convulse at its carnival invectives
A braying huckster cruelly reminding me
Of what was surely so
But can never be again.

Turning away
Instinct takes over
And I spin myself alone.

Suspended in my chrysalis tomb
I sway in the faintest breath of hope
And sleep the moon's enchanted dream
Of endless midnight beginnings.

A cantor's call of not-yet times
Cries out in the hundredth dawn
And I blink to full awakening.

When night's guardian stone rolls rightly away
In sentinelled sight of a new day's promise
I unfurl to first light's freeing warmth
And wing onto heaven's glory way.

Remembering Living

Flashing boldly through laureled gates of death
Soul knows itself fully once again
Within the gigawatt immensity of forever.

In the tremolo of Light's lucid laughter
It lets go personality's sole perspective
And finally gets the cosmic joke
Of agreed-upon limitation
Of let's-pretend not-knowing.

This is love's true coming home
When high heaven's exquisite shoulders
Shake with irrepressible mirth
While watching this again-remembering.

But we who remain on this side of the veil
Not recalling who we are or are becoming
Mourn deeply the passing that cuts life's link
And are burdened with the lifetime sentence
Of fictioned death's separation.

Bound by chains on now-caustic Earth
We go spinning into deeper, darker space
Trembling in dread of Death's kiss.

Then salvation comes.

The incomparable harlequined Fool
Bursts noisily through the self-sealed doors
Of grief's imprisoning isolation
And in the in-between pause of not-here awareness
Eternal knowing slips through.

It is for the living to let go the what-ifs
And the possibly-could-have-beens
To release the should-haves and hurtful why-nots
Of thundering incompleteness.

So that at pain's end and through its journeyed state
It will ultimately be the Earth-bound living
(And not the dead with no need of admonition)
Who can finally rest in peace.

Spawning

This mysterious, magical, almost-secret word
Conjures reminders of potent patterns
Of instincts too inherent to ignore
Of beingness too lusty to be denied
Unless gobbled asleep and summarily excreted
By those choosing to live unaware.

These bit players in their hackneyed dramas
Paying homage to the heart-numbing ordinary
And indulging in fake routine's inattention
Clutch possessively at their slow-death habits
To numb themselves and remain unconscious
As they stumble toward castrating inconsequence.

Wake up, all you trapped in narcotic illusion
That's not why you chose to be born
Decide to be dreamers—not just the dreamed
And spawn with those heeding the urgent call
To manifest our generational future.

Spawning.

It's time to reclaim the wondrous creaturehood
Of this humanly significant word
To feast on a moment of communal reminder
That we never swim alone.

We spawn, we die, we return once again
Remembering our born-with rhythms
In the glory of cycling renewal
In the majesty of mystic migration
We find our way back Home.

Spawning.

Reaching the Summit

For how many years did I seek to escape
The encroaching geography of his sheltering hills
Longing to navigate my own far pathways
And flee the tree-lined shores of predictable
    childhood?

The air trails of adolescence launched my flight
Then the grown-up conquest of a pretend wilderness
Which eventually spiraled my adult satisfaction
Until satiated, I called the game complete.

In ripened fields I discovered the nestling songs
Of my burgeoning trued-up rhythms
And lived in the immensity of unclocked time
Of unplanned pleasure and delight.

His dying froze my time and stopped the world
While recalling me to houred remembrance.

Suspended in love's deepening respect
I considered this one who had given me space
And from the swept-clean place of what-is-so
Reviewed our shared long-patterned memories
With sovereign equanimity.

I saw this mighty mountain of a man
Was but himself a singular mass
In an eon-long chain of immensity
And the succession of his fathering
Had birthed only the folded growing hills
Of my own time's ever-becoming.

In his passing, I stand as my own pinnacle
Anchored in circling seas of possibilities
Knowing the tectonic movement of life's each act
Has thrust me up to become my own mountain
My own generational. immensity.

Gazing into vision's guardian waters
I see echoed our dual reflections
Similar, yet separate
Mindfully, not duplicated
Gratefully, not mirrored.

For this is the now and eternal way
Of the tempered mountain people
This community from singularity
Holding true the high bright stations
Keeping faith with dusky evensong.

Messengers

This is the kind of lazy morning
When I would usually call my Dad
To tell him of inconsequential events
Which enrich my life replete.

I would tell him of the love-struck jay
Winsomely clinging to deckchair's back
And chirping lustily at windowed cat.

I would replay the sound of the hunting hawk
Swooshing into the quiet yard today
To capture a feeding finch.

I would warmly describe the peace I feel
And how amazed I am by the lovely life
Through which I buoyantly swim
Then I would thank him for the eyes he trained
To recognize the always-beauty of it all
Touched by the glorious Divine.

But now I will do so anyway
And express love to the father no longer here
By giving gratitude for inherited knowing
Fashioned by the complexities of everyday simple
Within the shared experiences of living.

So, transcending the bounds of space and time
I send this postcard Home.

Marking Returns

They have almost all gone now
This family of my youth
Those who hold my recollected history.

Some
Intent pilgrims on the fabled El Camino of death
Others
Wanderers in the wilds of emotional distance
All
Punctuating their palpable humid absence
In a cabaret of lively silence.

It is when these phantoms of remembrances
Ignore their negotiated boundaried space
That I tactfully reassert my treaty rights
And hold dear the truer trysting place
Within the circle of my interlaced lives.

Here, the meadow flowers brightly bloom
In festive disarray
Here, their now-and-forever sweetness
Is sipped by my lingering heart.

Counting Coup

In the respectfully silent browsing aisles
Of pre-life-to-post-death greeting cards
Trickster untethers mind's reason.

With the magical piping of his unvoiced flute
He makes fly my bound-up memories
Of life's tectonic traumas
And without hesitation or remorse
He forever rearranges my tamed inner landscape
And returns it to the wild.

The weeping weave of his Earth-bound song
Makes my tumble of lamentation more poignant.

How I miss the annual pageant-picking
In the search for a just-right card
Which express my heart's honoring message
To family and friends now gone
A confounding ache especially felt
For birthdays no longer enjoyed.

Then Trickster switches his doleful tune
To a jig of glad recollection
And I stand transfixed in gathering gratitude
For the greater number of those still living
Those adding a tilting affirming balance
To my sad reckoning of the lost.

Through his magical music I finally understand
The leaving-outs and more hopeful adding-ins
Of the edited list of commemorative moments
Generate their own electric atmospheres
Their own climatic consequences
Creating a treasured protected surround
Keeping my lovely labyrinthine life
Kindly green and growing.

I look up and find myself alone
Holding dear this harlequined gift
Wrapped in the plaid of reversed perspective
A carbonating injection of renewing hope
Botoxing my sagging world.

Emergence

My long-fixed path around this stellar orb
Has not yet completed itself.

Instead my light is still near-full eclipsed
Not yet shining with connected radiance
Of divinity's constellated mattering.

I grow impatient with this Saturnian passage.

What once was comfortable and aptly familiar
Feeding me so richly in its humid darkness
Has become too tight, too confining, too not.

Around the people of the dawn
I feel the pause the most
Those recently returned from the underworld
Initiated by Death's own hand.

Having experienced beginning's recalibration
Manifested by origin's designed integration
They now emanate resurrected Venus light
Shimmering with sustaining joy.

But my time has not yet come
And I anticipate soon-to-be springtime
In the almost-but-not-quite-yet
When I return as one reborn.

But a challenge voice shouts *it cannot be*
And drives me to examine true intentions
This inner voice living in forever lack
A mocking voice making me ever stronger
One I push against to bring the balance
Through an isometric flexing of the soul
Made firmly toned by my conscious response
Of a consistent *so I choose*.

The quickening of false labor ensues
But just enough to excite me
Just enough to threaten me
Just enough to let me know
My time is drawing near.

There is no command with fetal development
Just an unfolding of right-timed becoming
A progressive pulsing patterned growth
Of anticipated hidden life.

When the sharp insistence of inner force
Pushes the waiting child to freedom
From dark safety's connected space
A passage readied by blood-mixed water
And completed with air-sucking breath.

And so it is I await my prefigured hour
For eternity to deliver my newest-now
I am a nascent neutron craving change
A trusting starseed seeking deliverance
Ready to complete this labored birth.

DAWN

Dawn

Like the subtle first hints of spring after a long and bitter winter, dawn arrives after the deep night of death. The subtle lightening of the once-dark sky to softer, darker gray heralds the shift.

Years after my father's death when I read the poems about my own dawn, I was struck by all the allusions to birth, the watery unconscious, and rigidity giving way to new life. I sensed seeds planted by death had been steadily growing in unseen places way beyond my view. A process was taking place I was not yet ready to know consciously.

Your dreams will give you hints of your own new beginnings, so take time to examine them. Sit with them, look at them from all angles, turn them over in your mental hands. They will speak. Dream images are your mind's attempt to represent your deepest truths and are rich with meaning. The all-of-you truly wants this part-of-you to be happy again. A few of your expired beliefs may present themselves for reevaluation and repurposing.

At this point of the death process, you might be tempted to impatiently bypass the dawn and reach for the full light of day. You want to just be done with this time. But if you rush, you might miss an important step in this alchemical process of change and transformation. Be willing to wait for the dawn—to have death still visit from time to time. False dawns may take you temporarily back to night, but in their own way, they prepare you for the coming day when death's passage is behind you.

As dawn follows night, you will surely return to full living—to life after death—but first honor this not-yet-daylight period, trusting your new day is making its way toward you. Until then, discover what death still has to say to you and continue searching for and unwrapping its sancti-fied gifts. Hidden within are hints of new visions and new dreams, a renewed belief in what might be possible for you.

Curiously, you may also notice that energy once focused on your loved one begins returning to you, and dawn is the time to figure out what you're going to do with it. Be inspired by what others have done with their returned energy. Parents who have lost children through senseless tragedy sometimes use it to join causes or organize movements to make things better for everyone. Children who have lost parents utilize their returned energy to live their lives more consciously and creatively. What will you do with yours? How will you use this returning energy to make a difference in your life and perhaps the lives of others?

Everything changes little by little through just one action taken by one person at a time. Happily planting flowers in your garden can have as much consequence as governing a nation if your intention is clear. You don't need to change the entire world, but, if you choose, you can employ this sent-back energy to change *your* world. What might this look like for you?

Dawn is subtle. You sense daylight is coming but you cannot yet clearly see the shape it might take, and long shadows still hide emerging patterns. By design, death's new dawn continues to slow you down a little in order to give you time to integrate death's experiences before returning fully to routine. Trust is required—trust in your process and in the coming day. Dawn creates periods of rest and moments of solitude amid returning activity. Take advantage of them.

If you have honored death's process and accepted its gifts, old filters have been removed, and you begin seeing the world and your life differently. Like having the prescription of your glasses or contacts changed, you may need to adjust your vision to accommodate this new ability to see more clearly. The timing of this process is different for everyone.

Dawn also creates opportunities to fine-tune what you have learned—a process which could actually take years—but time does not matter. What is important is your willingness to take the first step in living a truer, bigger life. The preparations of dawn get you ready for the action of daylight.

When you begin moving into daylight and leaving death behind, you may be a bit disoriented as you slowly return to routine and still feel somewhat out-of-phase with those around you. You may notice unexpected emotions. Your loved one is gone. Doesn't the world care about that? Why does it keep functioning as it always has? Why does every-one expect you to simply pick up where you left off before death swept you away? Don't they know things can never be as they were?

However, though your outward form and routines may look the same to others and even give you comfort, you have been irrevocably changed. Perhaps you continue to feel awkward for a while. You might be tentative about integrating your experiences and figuring out your *new normal*. These are hints that during these times, you must be very kind to yourself.

Conversely, you might try so hard to return to the *old normal*, you aggressively reach for who you used to be before death, only to find your familiar self is missing. Use the brightening light of dawn for the *remade you* to begin determining what your expanded understanding of life demands.

Prepare for the coming day by first unfolding into dawn. Released from the grip of night, give thanks for the returning light. Trust that full daylight will follow the dawn.

Remember that experiencing death is a process you have now almost completed. Dawn is the time to call up your strength and find the courage to begin returning to life.

Dawn

Sun slowly slides horizon high
And rouses the slumbering silent.

Fog lovingly laps with soft caress
The hushed and dreaming hills.

The gorgeous Unseen walks here
Unbound and making sacred
Fulfilling origin's ever promise
Of perpetual resurrection.

Along this knoll-defining causeway
Spinning shadow-dancers beckon.

They wave misted fronds of hosannaed hello
And toss cloud-like kisses of welcome
Chanting hymns of mysteried moments.

Earth's quickened bloodlife swiftly responds
And salsas in crescendoing rhythm
As singers excite glad awakening.

Creation's canticles of harmonied awe
Call forth the stations of the day
Inviting all to awaken and play
With the swelling possible of the new
In the light of a pregnant dawn.

Breaking the Surface

Finally, there is movement.

I feared my heart's container would burn away
Before the sleep-charmed waters in its darkly depths
Spelled by the unknown turns of my finding path
Could bubble elatedly to the surface.

This inner tension formed a steeled seal
A blockade I railed against and resented
A taunting reminder of what-was-not.

As the heating waters moved upward
And shattered liquid's barriered cage
I realized this was not a lid on passion
Or prohibition against freer expression.

Once the ceiling irrevocably cracked
A hazy glow shined through
Dimly lighting the mysteried surround
And exposing to my marveling eye
The thin ovoid wherein I swam.

I touched an egg's all-shielding frame
Revealing not the shall-nots I so fiercely fought
But a shelled wombed wonder of tight protection
My maverick mind had failed to see.

Womb-like I was secured and warmly cradled
Growing suspended in love's gifting solitude
A brightening future gestating within.

Finally, there is movement
Being quickened by sacred intention
Within the blueprint of origin's design
My chick-self is prompted to grow.

I float in the embryonic waters
Of an elixired brew of new
A promise of the ordinary exotic
To hatch when the time is right.

Alleluia!
There is movement.

Brooding

In rebirth's nest I roost
And incubate true destiny's purpose
Sheltered in the animating mystery
Of this endlessly navigated journey.

The time of emergence draws near
When my hatchlings break free of shell
To unite with the already rhythms
Of their siblinged inner flock.

And when they finally wing in lifting flight
With sureness born of ancient promise
I will airily stretch new-feathered wings
To become the latest outer expression
Of my perpetually versioning self.

But today I patiently wait and watch
Trusting in life's appointed hour
When the resurrection call to arise
Bids me seek my birthed-new skyway.

In the now of this tithing time
I hold my hushed potentials warm
Alone in still-winter's dawn.

My process seems out of season
To those who observe and question
Since all my steadfast companions
Have long ago flown south
Not yet returned to prepare a nest
For their own next brooding time.

I ignore the watchers and guard the secret
Bound in narrow density's promise
Quickened by initiation's vows.

Keeping faith with my ever process
And gestating eternal tomorrows
I pulse in time with the pauses between
Knowing all is well with my world.

 Dawn

Times of Grace

The lights go on
And the heavens clap
The dimly directed
Become the blessèd ones.

Just like that.

Generating Energy

For years I held them reverently in my head
The ideals of honor, rightness, and valued living
But the diet grew tedious with its repetitive fare
And I hungered for an audacious alternative
An avenue to the beckoning panoply
Of temptation's epicurean delights.

In the dawn of a misted morning
In the secret time between silent worlds
I made a fateful belly-smacking leap
From high in my head to deep in my gut
And reinitialized the grand adventure
Of inspired emotional return.

Gaining lowering perspective to feel life raw
Diving deep into passion's pools
I crawled with greed and was sticky with lust.

I preened in the mirrors of my undervalued vanity
And finally reclaimed the gypsy parts
Of my heated humid humanity
The emotions lingering in the vast cathedrals
Of the circling subterranean dark.

In the cohabitation with the all-of-me
I found delicious delight in the shadows of light
In the secret entwining of hidden other.

Now having crossed continuum's vast extremes
And tarried at the dalliance points between
I hover Buddha-like on the summary middle path
Making godly soul choices to mark my passage
On the volatile emotional seas within
This endless rocking motion of tidal aliveness
This alchemical gastronomic process
By which my spirit is fully fed.

Getting Punk'd

I hear dragonflies are harbingers of change
So, what does this group have to tell me?

I watch as these five fly madly around
Like sky children joyfully cavorting
Forming an intricate webbing matrix
Of dizzying patterned consequence.

My eyes track their invisible contrails
Hypnotically pulling me deeper
When without warning or hesitation
Emanating the undreamed possible
A crack between the worlds appears
And unexpectedly rewires my brain.

I get the message.

Light's grace flows forcefully through
In a heaping flood of primal awakening
And suddenly, I remember.

God guffaws and is vastly amused.

 Dawn

Processional

Loosened tatters of bedrock beliefs
Chaotically blow askew
These forgotten and faded flags
Of kingdoms once imperiously ruled
Now whip in the heavied winds
Of crushing cruel inconsequence
Torn from a heart broken open
By the very living of life.

Coming undone
I am fiercely tender
With both my gladness and my terror.

Spirals of the mysterious and newly found
Sinuously entwine the lovely and always-known
Defining the rocketing almost-there possibilities
Wherein I slowly spin.

Shards of tumbled magical mirror
Once enchanting through stealthy inference
Now puddle in the luminous light
And reflect old dreams in need of slaying.

With altered perspective and a hint of squint
Recently formed patterns wink alive
Eagerly beckoning me to hasten through
The triumphed archway of Hallelujah.

Crossing the Vale

Peace, a pilgrim on life's sacred pathways
Carries within her light-tempered chalice
A transmuting draught of merciful unbinding
Which when sipped with choice-laced courage
Collapses corrupting fear.

Lately awakened and newly re-formed
I join peace-kissed kin of ingested redemption
Commingling my gratitude tears of compassion
Filling the prophesied pool of union.

Experiencing this hallowed deliverance
And immersed in its liquid benediction
I know a serene certitude of concordance
With the joy of the finally found.

Harbinger

Beware the light of this newest year
Oh, parts of me remaining hidden and secure.

Beware the bright of this adventuring time
Oh, inner minions clutching tried-and-true.

For I have thrown wide open the vine-green shutters
And the Fool is dancing down the street.

Beware his entrance into your settled domain
Because my heart is ready to cavort.

Pretend Wind

Blowing breathing beneficence.

What I thought of as the wind
Is really the playful exhale of God
Re-making me
Re-awakening me.

It couples with my human inhalations
In lungs' bronchialed latticed cathedral
Where the draw of each light-laced breath
Is vivified by spiritual rapture.

Swept Away

Christos consciousness of creation's fire
Raging unnoticed by the most
Welcomed and celebrated by the awakened
Tosses the alerted from their sleep.

The choice time is marked and unerringly gallops
Towards the crossroads of fated meeting
When fallacious fear falls fitfully away
And Earth emerges as one renewed
Changed and whole from her birthing passion
A mother who has delivered herself
As a maiden fine and fair.

In a galactic cotillion of coming out
With its pomp of soul's initiation
This newly remembering starseed
Is escorted to the spiraling dance
Whirling in circles of intricate design
To transform the orbiting worlds.

The Unknown

A head of steam in building
Of impatience and frustration
Of a greediness to finally know
Where all of this is going.

But I will not vent
I will not rage
I will not speak aloud
But simply allow this building pressure
And trust in life's transmuting process
Where the tough becomes the tender
Where the slow becomes the swift.

Then
When I am finally cooked
I will dine on this next-course feast
Prepared by the sumptuous Unseen
Artfully presented with a flourish and a wink
On gorgeous plates and crystal glass
In a gardened bower of delight.

The fare stimulates my questing taste
For what might be offered next
As I sip the rich red wine of restoration
And sing a freed-one's hymn of thanks.

The Couriers

It makes no difference.

Full moon to see by
Or sickle moon to guide me.

As I witness my life's clocked movements
In the star-framed sky of eternity
And track my waxing then fading wane
On the unknown's lunar chart
As an explorer, my confidence grows.

I can read the signs and portents
As the way comes more clearly known
And set the pace of unplanned progress
In exact and perfect timing.

In the meantime
I lay a silken blanket on carpeting grass
And scan for prophesied comets of change
Searching the multitude of diamoned lights
For the one to guide me to Bethlehem.

Timeless Tune

The remodeled song with its woofered percussion
Blazingly recalls youth's jukebox moment
When it first pounded my more innocent heart
With such ripping urgency and impossible passion
An apparently long time ago.

I stand transfixed by its evocative lyrics
Now temptingly beckoning my instant return
To a hopeful moment of forever springtime
In the garden of a butterfly world.

Song's rhythmic tutelage informs my knowing
It has fulfilled the caterpillar's cocooning promise
Made to my young one's immaculate yearning.

Then dripping chords, the tune withdraws again
After thanking me for my soul-spun dreaming
Leaving behind the ripened secrets
Of longevity's toe-tapping truths.

Gateway

Birds gliding artfully on morning's soft mists
Appear then disappear through green-leafed portals.

Zipping between the waiting worlds
They twitter cheekily to remind those too grim
To finally get the joke of it all.

In-Between Maybes

Sunday silence of a mid-winter afternoon
Falls like invisible mists over the relaxing land
Then rises again to mute the scavenging mind
Locked in echoing memory of summer.

What was begun is truly over
And the next, an unimagined hint
As I drift in the pause of the ever possible
And dream of nascent tomorrows.

Gestation

Held softly in the sac of the sacred
Deep within the belly of the Earth
I find peace in my solitary existence
Pulsing, pulsing, ever pulsing
In the tendering heart of the Divine.

Unmade and remade
All-formed and re-formed
Breath quickens me
Light excites me
And when I finally emerge as other
As a felicitous mutation of what-if,
I will embody the infinite I Am.

The time of my return is near.

I thrill with an electric trembling
As spirit strums my spine
Tickling my imagination.

My muse stretches towards the sun
Demanding expression's birth
Challenging me to repaint my life
In gratitude's primary colors.

Resurrection

Sweetened by sun
Fructified by moon's largesse
The tidal influences of oceanic amplitude
Stir my body with ancient remembrances
And swizzle-stick me to excitement.

This ancient mixology of remaking
Comes with a bright umbrella of joy
A happy margarita of invention
To celebrate the almost-time.

Taking Flight

At first
I flew only at night
Because I could easily pretend to my day-self
I was simply dreaming.

Then I stopped play-acting and told myself the truth
But continued to fly only in remote places
Where I would surely remain unseen.

I thought my flying would appear rather freakish
An embarrassment to the tribe
So, I closely guarded my secret identity
Just in case and against all odds
I just happened to be a superhero.

When I learned there were others who flew
I instantly felt less alone
But was still afraid of being shot down
By those who thought I was a gamebird
Or something far less obvious.

I finally tried teaching my friends to fly
Thinking this would bring credibility
And I could barter for acceptance.

But this didn't work and I stopped trying
Trusting in my friends' own dreamtime
To awaken them to flight.

Now I fly because I love to fly
And explore the acrobatics of it all
By searching out multi-spaces
And seeking out plenty-times.

I suppose one day soon I will be joined by others
Because more and more as time goes on
I see solitary flyers coasting in their dreaming
But only in remote places
And only when they mistakenly think
That no one else is watching.

I gratefully acknowledge Brian Andreas and his verse,
"Flying Woman," 1993, as the inspiration for this poem.

Lovely Reluctance

The wily wind flirtily rises and falls
Hurrying first fruit's white-starred blossoms
In circling pirouetting partnership
With even whiter cold-tipped snow.

This is mystery's in-between time
When the closed-tight fist of wavering winter
Slowly unfolds finger by reluctant finger
To reveal budding, sleeping spring
Who barely stretches and sweetly yawns
Before pushing time's fail-safe snooze button
To dream just a little more.

Is it winter?
Is it spring?
Ultimately, the choice is mine
To which will I offer my heart's allegiance?
For which will I sing my song?

DAYLIGHT

Daylight

DAYLIGHT FOLLOWS NIGHT. IT IS INEVITABLE, AND IT is the way of things. Though the day dawns cloudy and gray, the lightening of the sky is still apparent, and even a dark day can produce moments of brightness. Daylight is the time your dreams can take on qualities of new life and renewed possibility.

Returning to the full daylight of routine is the final step in the death process. However, as you began experiencing at dawn, you might notice that with changed perspective comes a new way of interacting with the usual and familiar. Perhaps you find old routines have become too limiting or painful for you and you adjust them, making changes which out-picture your bigger, stretched-out perspective. Or perhaps you stay within old routines, but they automatically are transformed because you are now more authentic and require different expression.

The experience of daylight is different for everyone, but what is common for those who have consciously and willingly embraced death's process, is the sense of waking up to a larger world. Most feel a sense of relief and usually, gratitude, at being on the other side of grief, but not everyone. Some might never integrate the experience into a more meaningful context for living, but the potential to do so is always there.

Death invites you to make your own process consequential. As with any journey, you can replenish yourself when it is complete and acknowledge the personal strength and courage you called upon to arrive at its end.

Daylight invites you to re-engage in full living and leave death behind, though you never actually abandon what it has taught you. You might choose to ignore the learning or push it away, but this new knowing is always there, waiting for you to explore its bounty. But be easy with your timing. You may finally understand when you're sixty what the death you experienced at twenty-five actually meant.

Daylight is not the time to feel guilty as you move on with life. Those who have passed beyond death now enjoy a truer state of existence and, if you could ask, loved ones would say they hope you use their death to live your life with richer meaning. Whether here or beyond, they want you to be happy.

Their deaths can become their final gift. You can open it, hide it, or give it away. Your choice. However, if you wish to truly honor them, use the timing of their gift to become different. Take more pleasure in life. Allow the transformation. Embrace the bright light of day—generous and overflowing, ripened and juicy. Then simply shine the new light which now fills you. You may be surprised and gratified by what you see.

Daylight

In a secret unvoiced inner space
It felt almost like betrayal
The world continued as it always had
Didn't they know he had died?

In a secret unvoiced inner space
I wondered at my audacity
How could I possibly enjoy my life again?
Didn't I care he had died?

But in the grand design of living things
With its endless ebbs and flows
With its undulating wilds and calms
Darkness passes
Daylight arrives
And life's urgent contractions of moving beyond
Always birth us alive once again.

But for me this is a changed alive
A more significant alive
A more attuned alive
Because after all, he had died
And gifted me with his legacy
A lush landscape of what is possible.

A legacy seeded at conception
Grown with kind care and attention
Brought only recently to flower
By my many grief-torn tears.

They fertilized the fecund ground
He left behind in time-bound death
And brought forth into the here-and-now
Season's riotously bloomed significance.

Budding eternity now perfumes the air
Wrapping my every breath in reminder
To use in full and plentied measure
Death's grief-gift claimed when he left
By dancing more amorously with Life.

So, with blossoms entwined I spin released
Seduced by evocative fragrances
Drenched in my body's sweet sweat.

I partner gracefully with piloting soul
Who takes me to Mystery's garden
Where I am planted in a bolder bed
Of more colorful complex design.

Blooming, I turn toward the Light
Enjoying this ripened time of amplitude
Embraced by the warmth of renewing gratitude
Rooted deeply in the endless sacred.

His death is a marker along my way
A reminder that within this ever-cycling space
I too will fertilize Earth's welcoming soil
And having scattered my seeds to the many
While trusting they can grow in a few
I will complete my own legacied era
And tango happily through heaven's door.

Changing Perspective

I release the strands of lighted morning
And fly aloft on rosy winds
Soaring high in jetted incandescence
On skies scrubbed clean of clouds.

Tucked safely into creatured remembering
I become the gliding red-tailed hawk
Endlessly hunting the far-faded memories
Of spindled unraveling
Of timely release.

Leaving behind the courageous maps
Defining both my heaven and earth
I willingly test the limitless boundaries
Of freed imagination's wondering
As I walk the golden honeyed maze
Of certainty's uncoiling metaphors.

Reaching the center of an ever-cycling center
I spread my mottled feathered wings
Over the unveiled vastness of becoming.

Then uttering the primordial word of potency
I turn homeward once again
Where with the conviction of a remembered
    immortal
I speak my world anew.

Directional Navigation

Rocking hammock-like through indecision
First saying *yes*
Then knowing *no*
Cushioned comfortably by the certain knowledge
That in a lively moment of stillpoint paradox
Embracing both polarities and all journeys
    in-between
I will know
Simply smile
And once again move on.

Heaven on Earth

What defeats me is not the aching absence
Of life-affirming relationships
But my death grip on breath-stopping isolation
Hurling me like a solitary satellite
Into the cold of deep-space inconsequence.

I know it's my invincible human heart
Which can shine the thawing light of mutuality
And illuminate this sham of repressive singularity
By breaking these chains of aloneness.

So, I open my heart to the underlying mystery
Flowing into the space of holy possibilities
Transporting me to my center.

Salvation begins.

On the altar of my truer self
I sacrifice learned separation
Before traversing the awaiting bridge
To my own divine rebirthing.

Standing near edge of darkened pool
I toss my pebbled choice for oneness
Into the very center of the silent stillness
And watch as ripples alter the shifting shores
Reaching beyond my tiny bounded space
Into the expanse of the forevermore
To join the expanding All.

Spirit awakens and reaches for Light.

The impact of this fateful intersection
Changes the very spinning of the Earth
As I reboot and come again online.

With channels opened and circuity complete
I rejoin the dimpled song of harmony
Heaven's high hosanna of glad resurrection
Draped in the glory of remembered connection
Individual and all
Ever-changing and immutable
Awash in creation's first Word.

Making a Way

There is a spangled wonder to not knowing
A pre-Christmas excitement for what's next.

Like following a trail of light-lit crumbs
In the dark of the deepest woods
I scavenger from place to place
Seeking treasures just beyond.

I've heard that it is not the goal
But the present journey which matters
And maybe this is mostly true
For those of singular road.

But I travel the maybe paths of what's possible
Often following no footpath at all
Trusting only an intuited at-birth promise
I'll come safely to the next site of rest.

Arriving, I refresh at the waiting feast
And enjoy my completion moments
But do not linger in this amiable space
Which could possibly seduce me with certainties
And sedate me with its comforts.

My destiny is to seek once again
The awakening of the multi-places
Those unmapped dimensions beyond tight time
Revealed by an unbarred heart.

So, I push away from the laden table
And dress freshly in temporary clichés
To be exchanged for truer perspectives
At the next found pausing-point.

I raise a last glass in the banqueting hall
And dispense wisdom to the needing young
Giving thanks for companions both far and near
Who no longer share my travels.

Emancipated, I walk into the swept-clean day
Feeling the hum of my electrified spirit
And heeding the call of the galactic winds
I continue curiosity's quest.

The Morning After

Within my diver's deep half-sleep
I hear my name twice called
And reluctantly reawaken
To another day's full promise.

I cannot fathom this brassy summons
From drowsy interlude following feasting
When the world digests life's bounty
And slumbers well past dawn.

Opening the darkening shades
I stand stunned by nature's largesse
And greedily devour luminescent opulence
Sparkling from high-knifed hills
Sailing among steeled-gray clouds
Of liquid possibilities.

Hastily tossing on coat and gloves
I race to chase their shadows
And in the quiet of a trade-wind morning
Vanish into moving mists.

Dissolving the boundaries between the worlds
I dance a dervish of thanks.

Catching Waves

What can I name this journey?
This high-speed marathon
Run without the distracting drama of what-if angst
Or the binary commotion of the tritely everyday
Mimicking awakened soul's true passion.

Instead I choose the vagaries of the surfer's world
With its exhilarating highs and its death-defying
    lows
And allow my practiced balance
To define this Light-flecked ride.

Perhaps it's best I cannot contain
These giant swells of my experience
Within the diminishing boundaries of words
So, I simply revel in this oceanic escapade
And dance with the dreaming dolphins
In the orb of the waxing moon.

No longer motivated by the terror of the unknown
(I have lived in these changing waters far too long)
I am now directed only by vast curiosity
And consciously honed true preference.

I seek the high magic of the always possible
Secreted in each wiped-clean day
And on a well-waxed streamlined surfboard
Race the sun to grand adventure.

The Search

We're eternal companions all to all
Though we might not yet understand this
As we continue delighting in imposed separation
While hungering secretly for the whole.

We are a pulsing sea of possibility
Fed by an ocean of galactic headwaters
Flowing furiously through space and time.

We forget that our magnificent thirst
Can be forever satisfied
By simply turning our collective head
To sip in wondering gratitude
The life wherein we float.

Birthed on a Carousel

I am the sole voyeur of my silent beginnings
The solitary traveler on these shifting tectonics
Which with unfathomable oceanic upwellings
Release the richly riotous rapture
Of time's incandescent knowing.

I function in familiar day's routine
And cause no startling wake in the tidal pools
Spelling the comforting geography of most.

My forays go unnoticed
My passages are unrecognized
Except by the few awakened ones
Who have sailed beyond their dragoned boundaries
And bear the initiated mark of trued-up explorers
On the circling calliope of wisdom's round
Spinning far beyond waiting stars.

Songs

There is a living hum to all things noticed.

Even the far echoes of tempoed traffic
Lull like lovely lushing waves
Lapping languidly on the resting shores
Of harmoniously hued inconsequence.

Indolent and happily idle
I nestle deeply within time's moments
Woven webs of colorful contrasts
Sacred and irreverent
Plodding and ecstatic
Soundless and strident
Encouraging my dance with soul.

Swaying to the rhythms of my pulsing blood
Charged by zipping neurons of electric body
My awakened senses frolic with the forever
And caper within defining human bounds
Enjoying boisterous tambourined interludes
In a dance of transcendent returning.

In the hum of rush
In the hum of peace
In the hum of life itself
I recall the music of I Am
And again, sing myself alive.

My Friends

At this time beyond all times
I string like hand-knotted pearls
On a seeded strand of lengthening light
The rewrites of my life
Quickened through the brightening eyes
Of my celebrating soul.

Secreted through the itch of life
Another pearl silently forms
Nourished by tides of unending time
And splendid moments of essential chaos
Redolent with perfumed grace.

As the tempo of urgency quickens
I give birth to my newest self
And lean into the sheltering love
Of those finding breath with me.

Those who inhale my discomfort
And exhale my hope
Who laugh at my nonsense
And make real my thoughts.

Those who stand with me
For me
Around me
My friends
Who carefully catch my crowning head
And pull me ever into joy.

My friends of the sacred circle
Shaped by the laughter of God.

Stellar Creations

Having preternaturally rhumbaed
With light's holographic wonder
Only creation beyond the tritely seen
Now manages to please me.

I am the architect of the new
I am the vessel of time's mattering.

With a command of wondering power
I spin the paths of far-flung stars
As they incubate in singing spheres
And witness scores of panting planets
In their gloriously rainbowed selves
Giving birth to the fabled beauty
Of imagination's soul-sourced species.

I reach inside my benedictioning heart
And grab a spilling of love-dust awakening
To sprinkle with stunning profusion
Their impatiently emerging progeny
In a baptism of possibilities.

The universe applauds in co-creative welcome
And scents the moment with perfumed flowers
A timeless celebration of the fecund and becoming
In the consummated truth of forever.

Flying to Paradise

Where does this enchanting spray
Of impertinently pink happiness come from
Mischievously squirting me with giggles?

I spin around and notice a shimmer of air
A shift in the settled usual
Curious but cautious, I expectantly watch
Sensing something is about to happen.

Suddenly the thinned-out fabric of what-is-here
Reveals an intriguing gateway to what-is-there.

With eager haste, the door crashes open
And I tingle as excitement builds.

Life as I know it stops.

Bounding into this suspended moment
The teasing Trickster smiles and bows
Cocking an eyebrow in assumed invitation
He nods to purposed portal.

I gladly stand and follow.

Chuckling gleefully at my childlike delight
He theatrically lifts the transparent veil
Of humanity's agreed-to forgetting
Revealing a marquee of lighted truths
Efficiently blanked out at birth.

Remembering, I fall to my knees.

No thunderous clap of sky-wide warning
No slow-motion play of muscle-tensed drama
Just a toe-curling gasp of redeeming recollection
As my heart meets the One-in-All.

I am eternally transformed.

Filled with a massive surplus of gratitude
I make my own respectful bow
As the angelic Trickster cheerily departs
Leaving the gift of memory behind.

Time returns to its usual flow
And I revert to ordinary sensing
Not really the same but forever alert
To the likelihood that at any moment
I will stumble into the surprising fantastic.

Unbridled Play

Licentious I want to be
Though not in the narrow moral sense.

Licentious.

To finally allow myself to explore,
With full license to wander freely
The wild byways the hedgerows hide.

License to live unbound
To sprawl willfully on gilded couch
Of silken opportunities
License to choose brocaded partners
Themselves, also licentious.

And then I will gladly and freely relinquish
The relentless need to hunt down and bag
The permissioned licenses of the always known
And by empowered command return my world
With words igniting and creating anew
The surprise of sweet origin's intent.

The Banquet

I always used to gulp life down
Never getting enough
Always wanting more
Exhilarated by the pursuit and the having
Drunk with the experience of needing.

Now I touch each squirming moment
To the tip of my awakened tongue
And I pause
More to imagine than to savor
(For savoring might chase just one result)
And rekindle mindful fruity visions
Of possibility's mysteried arroyos
Pathways to the many ways.

Standing in enfolding silence
Within these quivering shape-shifting truths
I watch as truer patterns emerge
To show me the way ahead.

Stepping onto this creational path
Of grander, greater freedom
I halt yet again with senses alive
This time, to fully taste.

In a fulcrumed swallow of prime-time gratitude
I let slide this sensual slice of life
Savoring my incarnated physicality
Wrapped tightly in divinity's dough.

EPILOGUE

EPILOGUE

After making the journey of death after my father died, I was different. Perhaps the recognition of my own mortality was the secret ingredient making this experience unique, but I don't think that's all of it. I had been through death before. My handling of the first important adult death in my life was messy, but I learned—about love, commitment, myself, my inner process, and about death. With each death, I became more attuned and better able to respond to the stages of grief.

Elizabeth Kubler Ross, a Swiss-American psychiatrist, in her landmark book, *On Death and Dying*, offered a roadmap to help the dying understand and manage their own stages of grief: *Denial, Anger, Bargaining, Depression*, and *Acceptance*. This model became the gold standard from which other models were developed since the book's publication in 1969.

A popular, widely accepted model derived from the original Kubler Ross process is the SARAH model: *Shock, Anger, Resignation, Acceptance*, and *Hope*. This model suggests a framework for understanding both personal grief and the grief of others during the death process. The SARAH model continues to be taught at universities and medical schools throughout the world and has endured because it accurately describes the human experience of us all.

Remember that death does not mean just physical death, but any significant ending causing us and our worlds to change. We go through the same SARAH process when we grieve the death of an individual, life stage, or event. Think about a big change you made, especially a quick and sudden change, and reflect on how you went through each stage of the SARAH death process. How did an old part of your life die to make way for the new?

This change process happens to us in the happy times of our lives as well, though usually not as dramatically. When you are married, it is important to first pause to respect and mourn the single status you are leaving behind. When the first baby comes, you leave behind a unique relationship with your partner. Or, you are offered your first management position and leave behind the people who might view with distrust anyone wanting to get ahead. It may sound strange to mourn what is no longer there, especially if the occasion is joyful and you have longed for this new beginning. But taking the time to process the passage—even if the mourning takes only an hour—can accelerate the time spent in finding the balance with your changed, more desirable circumstances.

What is important to keep in mind is grief is not linear. You may arrive at *Acceptance* only to find that *Anger* roars to the foreground again. Your process may take several weeks or perhaps even years. Everyone and every death is unique, so let that be okay with you.

Endings and changes can be unexpected and jarring whether perceived as positive or negative events. But physical death is a different matter.

Death is a predicted visitor who arrives at unanticipated moments. I first met death when I was very young and a cousin died with whom I had an unusually strong bond. Though I could not verbalize the inner trauma I felt, this was my initial experience of the void—of *gone and never again*—though I did not even know what that meant. I just knew death was terrible.

Eventually, I learned that since I would be hosting death from time to time, I had better become better acquainted with who death is and what death demands. Since then, there have been multiple deaths and visits from death with different degrees of personal impact, and death has become more familiar. I have learned to honor the role death plays and have received death's gifts. My sincerest hope is that when this one comes to escort me Home, I will finally greet death as a friend.

Remember that the death process can be a transformational journey. Let it be what it is. Respond in your own highly personalized way by being present to your feelings and validating their authenticity.

Throughout the process, others will offer counsel and comfort, but death is a solitary journey customized by your soul to help you grow into your true greatness. You may stop and be refreshed at the waysides of love and encouragement along death's pathway, but always, you alone determine how you will take this journey. Don't ignore the gifts death brings.

We all grow and change at different rates at various times. Perhaps you can now open yourself to decades-old deaths which you were not able to deal with previously. Grief's greater wisdom has no expiration date and is always there when you wish to accept it. Again, don't ignore the gifts death brings.

Peace will follow. This is life's promise to those willing to cooperate with it and continue to learn, grow, and change. When you wait with trust and hope, when you keep faith with yourself and your process, when you can still get excited about what life will bring you next, the customized gifts of bountiful grace are always given.

With courage, be confident that all is truly well whether you understand it yet or not. With courage, live your life. With courage, continue to love.

May your heart always know the kindness of peace.

A Life with Peace

When I was a toddling fledging child
She embraced me
And solemnly introduced herself as Peace
Trusting, I knew her wholly
As safety and belonging.

We played in the green-washed dells
Of imagination's innate wonder
And sparked each other with stuttering courage
Always dreaming of what would be.

She matched me inch by inch as we both matured
While when gathering time's delights
We explored the gapping space
Between grown and not-yet-grown.

Peace was mischief and adventure then
And without hesitation
We swam on beckoning breezes
And buds of being-right surety
While tentatively seeking our freedom.

In the teenage years
Peace came as freedom from
From the shrill admonitions of *must not*
From the annoying rat-a-tat-tat of *be careful*
But we paid no heed.

Into gleeful heights and thundering depths
We journeyed the wild ride
In an ever-creating crescendo of awakening.

In the fast acquiring years
Somehow
Without even remembering when it happened
I lost track of Peace
Family, job, and I came first
Peace was a staid reminder
And I was busy building a life.

Then in a distanced time
In deep night's slowed-down rhythm
I dreamed of Peace.

She was dramatically draped in mythic purple
And whispered seductively of what-if potentials.

Peace, the temptress
Offered me powdered lines of power I eagerly
    learned to snort
And I coveted the always more-of-more with
    pirated intensity.

In this heat
With regulated rigor and coveted re-consequence
I recrafted all of life
And fit it to my will.

I became a container for my own bounty
Overflowing and ripe, succulent and full
For Peace was now plentitude and harvest.

When my storehouse was full and my life replete
Peace became an annoyingly persistent caller
Throughout the tumbling together of those
    remembered years
She would carry the sharp tang of urgency and
    pin-pointed need
And by these two qualities did I know her.

This needy Peace drew freely from my reserves
For Peace beyond all else is pragmatic
There was work to be done
There were ministries to be reborn.

It is twilight now
And in wisdom's parlayed time
We rock quietly on the sheltering porch
Peace and I
Watching the flaring finality of sun-soaked sky.

Here is meandering comfort and rest
And once again
I know Peace as safety and belonging.

Contentedly I look at Peace
And stretch out my aging hand
Speckled with fulsome gratitude.

At this journey's end
In the settled satisfaction of large promises made
    and kept
I take Peace into my heart
And know myself for the first time again.

Acknowledgements

⬥

Looking back, I must again express deep gratitude to family, friends, and well-wishers who supported me through all my journeys with death and helped me heal. This is especially true during and after the death of my father, and I especially thank my brother, John Michael, for ferrying my father so lovingly and deftly through the final death process.

I did not ask my usual *Fab Three* readers to review this poetry book (though they were more than willing) because this journey was highly personal, and I simply wanted them to read the poems afterwards as a complete experience. Thank you to Rae, Sharon, and Anne for understanding this and for not rolling their eyes after listening to my somewhat convoluted rationale for not reading the book in advance.

I also decided not to reach out to other potential readers as poetry is not for everyone, and I did not want to guilt-trip them into an exercise they might find tedious. Thank you, potential readers, as always, for your willingness. However, since I know that poetry usually finds its way into the listening hands of those who would enjoy it and grasp its messages, I am comfortable with my decision.

Finally, I give another shout-out to the team at Luminare Press who continue to impress and exceed my every expectation. Patricia, Claire, and Kim, you're the best! Thank you.